6. Pray for God's help. You *need* God's help in order to understand what you study in the Bible. PSALM 119:18 would be an appropriate verse for you to take to God in prayer.

7. *Class teachers using this course for group study will find some helpful suggestions* ~~ ~~~~ 63.

how to
take the self-che

Each lesson is concluded with a test designed to help you evaluate what you have learned.

1. Review the lesson carefully in the light of the self-check test questions.

2. If there are any questions in the self-check test you cannot answer, perhaps you have written into your lesson the wrong answer from your Bible. Go over your work carefully to make sure you have filled in the blanks correctly.

3. When you think you are ready to take the self-check test, do so without looking up the answers.

4. Check your answers to the self-check test carefully with the answer key given on page 64.

5. If you have any questions wrong, your answer key will tell you where to find the correct answer in your lesson. Go back and locate the right answers. Learn by your mistakes!

apply
what you have learned
to your own life

In this connection, read carefully JAMES 1:22-25. It is only as you apply your lessons to your own life that you will really grow in grace and increase in the knowledge of God.

The First Coming of Christ Foretold

The story of the Bible is: "The Lord is coming." Both Old and New Testament believers have been cheered by the prospect of a soon-coming Christ.

Christ's first coming was foretold in detail

Listed below are a number of Old Testament predictions concerning the coming Christ, together with the New Testament fulfillment of each.

1. In what way was the Lord's birth to be unique?

ISAIAH 7:14; MATTHEW 1:21 _____

_____

2. Where was Christ to be born?

MICAH 5:2; MATTHEW 2:5, 6 _____

3. Of whom did the first prophecy in the Bible speak?

GENESIS 3:15; GALATIANS 4:4, 5 _____

4. How was Christ's forerunner described?

ISAIAH 40:3, 4; MATTHEW 3:3 _____

_____

5. By whom was the Lord to be betrayed?

PSALM 41:9; ZECHARIAH 13:6; MATTHEW 26:49-58 _____

_____

6. For how much was Christ to be betrayed?

ZECHARIAH 11:12; MATTHEW 26:14, 15 _____

_____

7. How was the betrayal money to be spent?

ZECHARIAH 11:13; MATTHEW 27:3, 7-10 _____

_____

8. Of what character were the witnesses against the Lord to be?

PSALM 35:11; MATTHEW 26:59, 60 _____

9. How was Christ to be ill treated?

ISAIAH 50:6; MATTHEW 26:67 _____

_____

10. What was Christ to say to His accusers?

ISAIAH 53:7; MATTHEW 27:12-14 _____

11. What mode of execution was foretold?

PSALM 22:16; LUKE 23:33 _____

12. How would Christ react to those who slew Him?

ISAIAH 53:12; LUKE 23:34 _____

_____

13. What mocking gesture would the bystanders make at Christ's execution?

PSALM 109:25; MATTHEW 27:39 _____

_____

14. What would the mockers say as Christ died?

PSALM 22:8; MATTHEW 27:41-43 _____

_____

15. How would they further embarrass the Lord?

PSALM 22:17; MATTHEW 27:36 _____

_____

16. In what words would Christ give expression to His agony?

PSALM 22:1; MATTHEW 27:46 _____

_____

17. What was to be done with His clothes?

PSALM 22:18; JOHN 19:23, 24 _____

_____

18. What would be given Christ to drink?

PSALM 69:21; JOHN 19:29 _____

19. Where would His friends stand?

PSALM 38:11; LUKE 23:49 _____

20. Though His death was to be a violent one, what was to happen to His bones?

PSALM 34:20; JOHN 19:33-36 _____

21. What significant fact is mentioned about His heart?

PSALM 22:14; JOHN 19:34 _____

_____

22. What was to be done to His side?

ZECHARIAH 12:10; JOHN 19:34 _____

23. Although His enemies were going to make His grave with the wicked, how was God going to overrule His burial?

ISAIAH 53:9; MATTHEW 27:57-60 _____

_____

24. Could the grave really conquer Christ?

PSALM 16:8-10; MATTHEW 28:1-8 _____

The purpose of Christ's first coming

25. What is the very meaning of the name *JESUS* given to Him at His birth?

MATTHEW 1:21 _____

26. How was He acclaimed by the angels?

LUKE 2:11 _____

27. What did Simeon testify when he looked on Christ?

LUKE 2:28-30 _____

_____

28. For what purpose did Christ come into the world?

JOHN 1:29 _____

29. What were the Lord's own words?

MATTHEW 20:28 _____

_____

check-up time No. 1

What have you learned in this lesson? Review the lesson in the light of the self-check test below. Check carefully any questions you can't answer. Be sure you have filled in the blanks correctly. When you think you are ready, take the test without looking up the answers.

In the right-hand margin write "True" or "False" after each of the following statements.

1. It was prophesied that Christ would be born in Bethlehem. _____

2. The first prophecy in the Bible speaks of Noah. _____

3. It was predicted that the betrayal money would be spent on riotous living. _____

4. It was predicted that people would gamble for the Lord's clothes. _____

5. It was foretold that Christ would be given water from Jacob's well at His crucifixion. _____

6. It was prophesied that Christ's bones would be broken. _____

7. The name *Jesus* means "Saviour." _____

8. Simeon declared that he had seen God's salvation when he looked on the infant Christ. _____

9. Christ came to deal with the question of the world's sin. _____

10. Christ's forerunner was John the Baptist. _____

Turn to page 64 and check your answers.

The Second Coming
of Christ Foretold

The first time He came to earth, the Lord entered by way of birth (GALATIANS 4:4; MATTHEW 1:18-23). When He comes the second time, it will be in power and great glory.

1. Examine the following Scriptures and in the blank space check (✓) the ones which teach that Christ's second coming will be visible, literal and glorious.

a. MATTHEW 17:26 _____   b. MATTHEW 24:27-31 _____

c. MARK 8:38 _____   d. MARK 13:24-27 _____

e. MARK 13:32-37 _____   f. MARK 14:61, 62 _____

g. LUKE 9:26 _____   h. LUKE 10:27 _____

2. Examine the following Scriptures and state whether Christ's coming again will be in a spiritual sense only, or in such a way that He will be seen by the natural eye.

a. ACTS 1:9-12   b. MATTHEW 24:27
c. LUKE 17:24   d. LUKE 21:27
e. PHILIPPIANS 3:20, 21   f. I THESSALONIANS 4:16
g. I JOHN 3:2   h. II THESSALONIANS 1:7-10
i. REVELATION 1:7

3. Examine the following Scriptures and state whether there is a sense in which Jesus is spiritually present among believers now, even though His physical presence is in heaven.

a. JOHN 14:16, 17   b. JOHN 15:26
c. JOHN 16:7, 14   d. MATTHEW 28:20
e. GALATIANS 2:20

_____

Physically Jesus is absent from this world and present at the right hand of the throne (JOHN 17:4, 5). There is a glorified Man in heaven as Great High Priest of His people and Head of the Church (ACTS 7:55, 56; I TIMOTHY 2:5; HEBREWS 12:2; 9:24; ROMANS 8:34). He is one day coming back in the clouds of heaven when the Body, the true Church, is completed. Believers, who comprise this Body, are told to watch for Him.

4. Of what practical value is this expectation of the Lord's coming again?

TITUS 2:13; II PETER 3:11 _____

_____

I THESSALONIANS 4:16 _____

_____

MATTHEW 24:44-46 _____

The coming of the Lord is a truth of such importance that it is mentioned 318 times in the 260 chapters of the New Testament (on an average, that is, of once every 25 verses). It is also mentioned a great many times in the Old Testament and most of these references are to the coming visible glory of the Lord on earth.

8

5. What is to happen to all believers when Christ comes?

I THESSALONIANS 4:17; I CORINTHIANS 15:51 _____

_____

Since some are to be caught up "alive," it is evident that the second coming of Christ does not take place at the moment of conversion as some would teach.

6. Will the world be gradually converted to Christ, or will it be largely apostate at the time of His return? Examine the following Scriptures and state whether we are to understand by the Lord's coming, the gradual conversion of the world to Christ by the preaching of the gospel in this age.

a. MATTHEW 24:12, 24   b. LUKE 18:8
c. MATTHEW 24:38, 39   d. I THESSALONIANS 5:1-3
e. II PETER 3:3, 4   f. II THESSALONIANS 2:3
g. I TIMOTHY 4:1   h. II TIMOTHY 3:13; 4:3

_____

Since at His coming Christ will find the world largely under Satanic control, it is evident that the victory of Christian principles in the world cannot be what is meant by the Lord's coming.

7. Did the Lord instruct the disciples that His coming would certainly take place in their day?

ACTS 1:6, 7 _____

8. Did He hint that it might be some time before He would actually return in person?

MATTHEW 24:14; 25:5, 19 _____

9. Is Christ's kingdom to be established on earth as a result of the gradual spread of the gospel, or suddenly and with divine power from above?

Luke 17:24 _____

10. Will anyone be able to point to its gradual appearing?

Luke 17:20, 21 _____

Premillennialists believe the Bible teaches that Christ will return at the close of this present evil age *before* the Millennium (the thousand year reign of Christ on earth). They believe that it is Christ Himself, with His accompanying angels, Who will make a separation between good and bad, after which He will personally reign as King of kings on earth.

Postmillennialists believe that all things during this present age are moving irresistibly forward toward a golden age, and that man himself will, through religious teaching, the advances of science and education, succeed in converting the nations and purging society, and that Christ will not come until *the close* of the Millennium.

11. Did Christ believe that the world would be converted at the time of His second coming? Examine the following Scriptures and check (✓) those which would indicate that He expected the world to be in a terrible condition at His return.

a. Matthew 13:30 _____ b. Matthew 13:38-43 _____

c. Matthew 13:48-50 _____ d. Matthew 24:4-31 _____

e. Matthew 24:37-51 _____ f. Mark 13:5-27 _____

g. Mark 13:34-37 _____ h. Luke 12:35-48 _____

i. Luke 21:20-28 _____ j. Luke 12:54-56 _____

12. Since Christ is to come at the close of the Great Tribulation, would it appear that His coming is pre- or postmillennial?

MATTHEW 24:29-31; LUKE 21:24 _____

13. What will men be saying concerning the Lord's coming as that event draws near?

II PETER 3:3, 4 _____

14. Did the apostles believe that the world would be converted before Christ came again?

a. *Paul*: I THESSALONIANS 5:1-9; I TIMOTHY 4:1-3

_____

b. *Peter*: II PETER 2:1-8, 12-14 _____

_____

c. *James*: JAMES 5:1-8 _____

_____

check-up time No. 2

What have you learned in this lesson? Review the lesson in the light of the self-check test below. Check carefully any questions you can't answer. Be sure you have filled in the blanks correctly. When you think you are ready, take the test without looking up the answers.

In the right-hand margin write "True" or "False" after each of the following statements.

1. Christ's second coming will be in a spiritual sense only.   _____

2. Study of the Lord's second coming is entirely without profit.   _____

3. At the Lord's coming all believers will be caught up to meet Him in the air.   _____

4. The world is going to be gradually converted to Christ during this present age.   _____

5. The Lord Himself indicated there was a strong possibility that much time would elapse before His second coming.   _____

6. The Lord foretold that the conditions on the earth would be fearful just prior to His return.   _____

7. As the time approaches for the Lord's return, men in general will be expecting it.   _____

8. The writers of the New Testament are unanimous in teaching that conditions on the earth will be chaotic as the time approaches for Christ's return.   _____

9. Although the Lord is at present absent from the earth, His Spirit is here.   _____

10. The Lord refused to tell the disciples exactly when His second coming would take place.   _____

Turn to page 64 and check your answers.

 LESSON 3

Two Phases of Christ's Second Coming

The majority of those who hold the premillennial view of our Lord's return indicate two phases of this event. First He is coming *for* His own; then He is coming *with* His own.

1. For what are all believers waiting?

TITUS 2:13 _____

(Note: The word "and" separates two thoughts. The last phrase is literally "the appearing of the glory.")

These two phases of His coming are often referred to as the *rapture* and the *revelation*. These expressions are derived from the Greek words *parousia* meaning "personal presence," and the Greek word *apokalupsis* meaning a "complete unveiling and revelation." The division of the second coming of the Lord into two phases does not rest solely on the use of these two Greek words in the original text. A study of the passages where they occur will show that there are distinctions as to time, persons, places and circumstances that indicate two phases of the Lord's coming.

2. What did the Lord Jesus tell the disciples He would do after preparing a place for them?

13

JOHN 14:3 _____

The Greek expression for "receive you" is a strong one, meaning "to take away by force."

3. What will happen (a) to those who have died trusting Christ and (b) to those believers who are alive on the earth when Christ comes for His own?

I THESSALONIANS 4:16, 17

a. _____

b. _____

4. In what manner will believers be taken at the coming of Christ?

MATTHEW 24:40, 41 _____

Some believers are of the opinion that this event takes place at the end of the Tribulation and that it refers to the taking away of the wicked for judgment and the leaving of the saints on earth. However, the Greek word for "taken" here is the same as in JOHN 14:3 and there translated "receive you." It is also used in connection with the taking of a bride (MATTHEW 1:20).

Contrasts between the two future comings of Christ

5. There is a coming *for* the saints. Then there is a coming *with* the saints.

a. What was the word given to His own at the time of His ascension?

ACTS 1:10, 11 _____

_____

b. How did Enoch prophetically describe the Lord's coming with His saints?

14

JUDE 14 _____

_____

_____

6. The Lord is comimg for those who are *saved,* and then He is coming to deal with those who are *lost.*

a. How does Paul describe the Lord's appearing for the believers?

COLOSSIANS 3:4 _____ ___ ___

_____

In God's order, what is to take place in terms of resurrection, after the resurrection of Christ?

I CORINTHIANS 15:23 _____ ___ ___

_____

b. When the Lord comes to deal with the wicked nations, into what two classes will He divide them?

MATTHEW 25:31-33 _____

_____

What will all the peoples of the earth do when they see the Lord coming in power?

REVELATION 1:7 _____

_____

7. The Lord is coming to reward *the Church* and then He is coming to re-establish *Israel.*

a. What will be the basis on which the Lord will reward those who have trusted Him and served Him?

REVELATION 22:12 _____

When did Paul expect to receive his crown for service?

II TIMOTHY 4:8 _____

b. Who is to be with the Lord when He comes to re-establish Israel?

ZECHARIAH 14:5 _____

Then who will reign over the earth?

ZECHARIAH 14:9 _____

What will He do to Israel's foes?

ZECHARIAH 14:12 _____

_____

What will those do who live through the Tribulation but take no part in the persecution of Israel?

ZECHARIAH 14:16 _____

_____

8. The Lord is coming as the *Bridegroom* and He is coming as the *King*.

a. Who is espoused as a chaste virgin to Christ?

II CORINTHIANS 11:2 _____

How is the Church described in REVELATION 19:7, 8?

_____

_____

b. In what capacity will Christ come back to earth after the marriage supper?

REVELATION 19:11-16 _____

9. The Lord is coming as the *Morning Star* and He is also coming as the *Rising Sun.*

a. What were the Lord's closing words to the true Church?

REVELATION 22:16 _____

_____

b. Addressing Israel, in the closing of the Old Testament, how does Christ promise to come?

MALACHI 4:2 _____

_____

Will the Church go through the Tribulation?

This important topic can be touched on only briefly here.

10. What is the explicit promise of REVELATION 3:10?

_____

11. Are members of the body of Christ to experience in any measure the "wrath of God"?

I THESSALONIANS 5:9 _____

The word "salvation" here means "deliverance" (see II PETER 2:5-9). He will "deliver" as He did Noah and Lot. According to II THESSALONIANS 2:7, during this age the Holy Spirit is actively hindering Satan's attempts to climax iniquity on the earth. In MATTHEW 5:13 the Lord Jesus described His own as "the salt of the earth." One of the functions of salt is to arrest corruption. The Holy Spirit, working through believers, is constantly holding back the final consummation of wickedness.

12. What will happen when this restraint is removed?

II THESSALONIANS 2:8 _____

_____

check-up time No. 3

What have you learned in this lesson? Review the lesson in the light of the self-check test below. Check carefully any questions you can't answer. Be sure you have filled in the blanks correctly. When you think you are ready, take the test without looking up the answers.

In the right-hand margin write "True" or "False" after each of the following statements.

1. All believers are waiting for death. _____

2. At present the Lord is preparing a place for His own. _____

3. Believers will be suddenly and mysteriously absent from their secular occupations the moment Christ comes. _____

4. There is to be a close resemblance between the way the Lord left His own for heaven and the way He will reappear for them. _____

5. Enoch foretold the Lord's coming *with* the saints. _____

6. When the Lord comes to deal with the wicked nations, He will divide them into three classes. _____

7. The Church is described as a chaste virgin in the Scriptures. _____

8. The Lord's coming in connection both with Israel and the Church is described under the figure of the Morning Star. _____

9. At least part of the Church of God will experience "the wrath of God." _____

10. The presence of the Holy Spirit on earth today is restraining the forces of wickedness. _____

Turn to page 64 and check your answers.

Who Will Be Taken When Christ Comes?

There are those who teach what is called a "partial rapture," that is, only those with a high degree of spirituality will be taken when the Lord comes. The others will be left to go into the Great Tribulation, possibly to face martyrdom. It is claimed that Christ's coming is compared to the coming of a thief, and a thief comes for jewels only. It should be remembered, however, that the comparison of Christ's coming to that of a thief was used to emphasize the *unexpectedness of His coming* (REVELATION 3:3). Christ is not coming to take what does not belong to Him. He is coming for all those who are His.

The parable of the wise and foolish virgins

1. Who is to go in with Christ to the marriage?

MATTHEW 25:10 _____

2. At Christ's coming, certain ones are to be taken. How does the Scripture describe these?

I CORINTHIANS 15:23 _____

3. How does a person become one of the Lord's?

JOHN 1:12 _____

_____

_____

4. What did the virgins who were "ready" have with them?

MATTHEW 25:4 _____

19

5. What is the significance of the lamp?

PSALM 119:105 _____

6. What is meant by the oil?

ZECHARIAH 4:1-6 _____

7. Does every true Christian possess the Holy Spirit?

ROMANS 8:9 _____

8. What does the Bridegroom say to those He shuts out of the marriage?

MATTHEW 25:11, 12 _____

The Judgment Seat of Christ

At Christ's coming, believers will be summoned to His Judgment Seat to receive rewards for faithful service, or else to witness their works burned as "wood, hay and stubble."

9. Will any believers be missing from the Judgment Seat of Christ?

ROMANS 14:10-12; I CORINTHIANS 3:12-15; II CORINTHIANS 5:10

_____

10. What will characterize some of the Lord's people at the coming of Christ?

I JOHN 2:28 _____

A completed Body

11. The Church is the Body of Christ. How is this described by Paul in I CORINTHIANS 12:12-20?

_____

_____

12. What is Christ's relationship to the Church, His Body?

Colossians 1:18 _____ _____ _____

13. Will any members of that Body be missing when it is at last presented to Him?

Ephesians 5:27, 30 _____

Christians are to live holy lives

14. What is said to be necessary that we may see the Lord?

Hebrews 12:14 _____

15. Who is "made unto us . . . righteousness" (holiness)?

I Corinthians 1:30 _____

16. What is the believer to do in order to have this holiness of life manifested in his everyday behavior?

Romans 6:19 _____

_____

17. Can any person produce holiness of life by his own efforts?

Romans 3:10 _____

18. What was Christ made for us?

II Corinthians 5:21 _____

19. What have believers been made in Him?

II Corinthians 5:21 _____

check-up time No. 4

What have you learned in this lesson? Review the lesson in the light of the self-check test below. Check carefully any questions you can't answer. Be sure you have filled in the blanks correctly. When you think you are ready, take the test without looking up the answers.

In the right-hand margin write "True" or "False" after each of the following statements.

1. The way to become a child of God is through sincere efforts to do good. _____

2. The oil the virgins had in their lamps depicts the Holy Spirit. _____

3. Every true believer possesses the Holy Spirit. _____

4. Christ denies that He knows those who are barred from His wedding feast. _____

5. Some Christians will escape the Judgment Seat of Christ. _____

6. The Church is described as being related to Christ, as a body is to its head. _____

7. Some members of this Body will be missing when it is at last presented to Him. _____

8. No man can see the Lord without personal holiness. _____

9. Holiness of life can be produced only after years of self-denial. _____

10. Holiness of life is imparted to those who trust Christ. _____

Turn to page 64 and check your answers.

The Resurrections

There is to be more than one resurrection

1. What two resurrections are noted in REVELATION 20:4-6?

a. _____

b. _____

2. By how many years will these two resurrections be separated?

REVELATION 20:5 _____

3. Which is the "better" of the two resurrections?

REVELATION 20:6 _____

4. What is necessary in order to share in the first resurrection?

PHILIPPIANS 3:9-11 _____

The phrase "resurrection of the dead" is literally "out from among the dead," and this is the word that is used throughout of the first resurrection—the resurrection of the saints. When the believers in Christ arise, the bodies of the unregenerate remain in the ground until the close of the Millennium.

5. How many of those who have died will be raised bodily?

JOHN 5:28 _____

6. How did the Lord Jesus show that the two resurrections differ and what did He call these resurrections?

JOHN 5:29 _____

_____

The resurrection of believers

7. When will the saints be rewarded?

Luke 14:14 _____

8. Will both the living and the dead who have trusted Christ share in Christ's triumph over death?

I Thessalonians 4:16, 17 _____

9. What must one secure in this life if he is to have part in "the resurrection of life"?

John 5:24, 29 _____

10. What will happen to our bodies when Christ comes again?

I Corinthians 15:51-53 _____

_____

_____

11. Who alone, at the present time, has full immortality?

I Timothy 6:14-16 _____

12. What will the believer's resurrection body be like?

I John 3:2 _____

The resurrection body will far excel the body that died, yet it will be the same body or an outgrowth from it. There must be an identity of substance, otherwise it would not be "resurrection" (the rising of that which fell). There are evidently elements of it which cannot be destroyed or assimilated, and out of these elements which were our own, God can as easily form a new body as He fashioned a body for Adam out of the dust of the ground. It is really no greater miracle that we should live again than it is that we should live at all.

13. Is heaven to be a real place or simply a state of mind?

JOHN 14:2 _____

14. How is this final dwelling place contrasted with what we now have?

HEBREWS 13:14 _____

15. Under what other figure of speech does the Scripture present heaven to us?

HEBREWS 11:14-16 _____

The resurrection of the lost

16. Those who have died without Christ are to be resurrected also. How is this event described?

ACTS 24:15 _____

_____

17. Since the sinner must answer for his sins in the body through which he sinned, what strong warning does the Lord give?

MATTHEW 10:28 _____

_____

18. After sinners have appeared at the Great White Throne in their own bodies, what happens to them?

REVELATION 20:12-15 _____

19. How may one settle forever the question of which resurrection he will experience?

JOHN 3:18, 36 _____

check-up time No. 5

What have you learned in this lesson? Review the lesson in the light of the self-check test below. Check carefully any questions you can't answer. Be sure you have filled in the blanks correctly. When you think you are ready, take the test without looking up the answers.

In the right-hand margin write "True" or "False" after each of the following statements.

1. The two resurrections will be separated by a period of two thousand years. _____

2. The "better" of the two resurrections is the first. _____

3. Only truly saved people will share in the first resurrection. _____

4. The Lord Jesus carefully distinguished between the two resurrections. _____

5. When Christ comes again for His own, their bodies will be miraculously changed. _____

6. Heaven is simply a state of mind. _____

7. Heaven is depicted in Scripture under the figure of a city. _____

8. Those who have died without Christ will remain forever buried. _____

9. Sinners who die without Christ can expect a second chance hereafter. _____

10. The way to settle in which resurrection one will share is to put one's trust in Christ as Saviour. _____

Turn to page 64 and check your answers.

The Judgments

There are four principal judgments mentioned in the Scriptures.

The judgment of sin at the cross

1. For whose sins did the Lord Jesus die on the cross?

I PETER 2:22-24 _____

_____

2. What position does every believer in Christ enjoy?

ROMANS 8:1 _____

_____

3. How is the believer assured that his destiny will never come into question?

JOHN 5:24 _____

_____

4. Where are multitudes of believers already?

II CORINTHIANS 5:8 _____

5. What is the only basis for this salvation and this assurance?

JOHN 3:16-18 _____

_____

_____

The judgment of the believer's works

This judgment takes place after Christ comes for His Church.

6. For what must every believer stand before the Judgment Seat of Christ?

II CORINTHIANS 5:10 _____

The Greek word for "judgment seat" is *bema*, a tribunal of award. It has to do only with those who are saved, and it is a judgment, not upon the believer's person but his works. (For a discussion of the doctrine of Rewards see *Practical Bible Doctrine*, a course in this series.)

7. How many believers will be called before this Judgment Seat?

ROMANS 14:10 _____

8. What is Paul's exhortation in view of the coming resurrection of the saints and the rewarding day to follow?

I CORINTHIANS 15:58 _____

_____

9. If the Christian's service for Christ has been worthwhile, what will be the result?

I CORINTHIANS 3:11-14 _____

_____

10. If his works are worthless, what will happen?

I CORINTHIANS 3:15 _____

_____

11. If a believer's works are burned up, does that mean that he has forfeited his salvation?

I CORINTHIANS 3:15 _____

12. When does the rewarding of believers take place?

LUKE 14:14 _____

13. Is this at the same time as the Great White Throne Judgment?

REVELATION 20:7-12 _____

The judgment of the living nations

14. What class of people are to be judged when Christ returns in glory to reign on the earth?

MATTHEW 25:31, 32 _____

Note that there is no reference to any resurrection in connection with this judgment. The text reveals that it is "the nations" who are to be judged and that this judgment will take place when Christ returns *with* His saints in glory. Prophecy makes many references to a judgment of the wicked nations.

15. How does Isaiah refer to this event?

ISAIAH 34:1, 2 _____

_____

16. What "controversy" is especially involved?

ISAIAH 34:8 _____

This means a settling of the Jewish question.

17. On what basis will the nations be judged?

JOEL 3:2 _____

Bear in mind that Matthew's Gospel is addressed primarily to the Jew and that the sheep and goat judgment is recorded right after the prophecy of a Jewish tribulation (MATTHEW 24).

18. Who are those who at this time will be blessed of God?

MATTHEW 24:34-40 _____

_____

It is important to note that the word rendered "nations" in MATTHEW 25 is translated "Gentiles" 93 times, showing that a distinction is made between Jew and Gentile. Christ will separate the goats (literally "he-goats," proverbially wild, and a type of a rebellious nation in DANIEL 8), those who have persecuted the Jew, from those who have done all they could in the tribulation period to ease the sufferings of the Jews. The living nations will be judged on the basis of their treatment of the Jews in "the time of Jacob's trouble" (JEREMIAH 30:10-24).

19. When Christ comes to judge the nations, will there be a great number of people living on the earth?

ISAIAH 24:5, 6; 66:16 _____

20. What will happen to those nations which rule God out of their affairs?

PSALM 2:1-9; ISAIAH 63:6 _____

_____

21. What nation will have a hopeful outlook at that time?

JOEL 3:16, 17 _____

_____

The judgment of the wicked dead

22. How many years after the judgment of the living nations does this take place?

REVELATION 20:7, 11 _____

23. Does this judgment take place on earth among the nations?

REVELATION 20:11 _____

24. Where do the subjects of this judgment come from?

REVELATION 20:13 _____

_____

25. What must each unsaved person face in that day?

REVELATION 20:12 _____

_____

"The books were opened." Every thought, word and deed of man is recorded. "Another book was opened"—the book of life, the register of the saved of all time. Only those whose names are written in this book will escape the fearful judgment of the Great White Throne.

26. What will happen to all those who have never trusted Christ, the Lamb of God, for personal salvation?

REVELATION 20:15 _____

The important question for every reader to settle is this: "Is my name written in the book of life?"

check-up time No. 6

What have you learned in this lesson? Review the lesson in the light of the self-check test below. Check carefully any questions you can't answer. Be sure you have filled in the blanks correctly. When you think you are ready, take the test without looking up the answers.

In the right-hand margin write "True" or "False" after each of the following statements.

1. The believer in Christ is still in danger of condemnation.   _____

2. The believer's destiny will never come into question.   _____

3. At the Judgment Seat of Christ believers will have to give account of their behavior as Christians.   _____

4. Those who have rendered to Christ worthwhile service as believers will be rewarded at the Judgment Seat.   _____

5. If a believer's works are rejected he will lose his salvation.   _____

6. The nations of the earth are to be judged in respect to their attitude to the Jewish people.   _____

7. The nations which have repudiated God will come into severe judgment in a coming day.   _____

8. The judgment of the wicked dead takes place forty years after the judgment of the living nations.   _____

9. The judgment of the wicked dead will take place on earth.   _____

10. The wicked dead will be consigned to the lake of fire after their judgment has taken place.   _____

Turn to page 64 and check your answers.

What Happens to the Believer at Death?

1. Do the redeemed at death enter immediately into the final state prepared for them? For what are they still waiting as the final step in the redemptive process?

ROMANS 8:22, 23 _____

2. When does this final perfecting take place?

I THESSALONIANS 4:16, 17 _____

_____

It should be remembered that no believer has yet entered the final and glorified state, nor is any sinner yet said to be in the final hell. Neither class has yet been tried as to works.

3. For what does the saved spirit still wait?

PHILIPPIANS 3:21 _____

_____

4. What is involved in death?

JAMES 2:26; ACTS 7:59; LUKE 8:55 _____

_____

5. Because death destroys the physical brain, does it follow that the believer no longer has conscious thinking power when he dies?

I Corinthians 2:11 _____

The brain is not the source of thought and will, according to the Scripture. Since it is the spirit, not the body, that thinks, wills, plans and holds communion with God, it follows that man's continued existence after death is not dependent on the body.

6. What happens to a believer when he is "absent from the body" at death?

II Corinthians 5:6-8 _____

7. What assurance did Jesus give to the believing dying thief in the hour of death?

Luke 23:42, 43 _____

There are those who teach that the word "spirit" used in Scripture simply means "breath" and that as soon as one stops breathing he sinks into total unconsciousness until the resurrection day. Examine I Thessalonians 5:23; Acts 7:59, 60 and Luke 8:55 to see that this is not the meaning. The spirit is the real personality which dwells in the body as its house. A *man* may be in his body or out of his body, according to II Corinthians 12:3, 4.

8. What is said in Psalm 115:17?

_____

This verse is often quoted to prove that the dead cannot serve and praise the Lord. The verse taken in its context (see verses 16-18), however, is dealing with God's cause *on earth*, not future existence. Such verses cannot be used to set aside the plain statements of the whole of Scripture as to future existence.

9. Does Scripture distinguish between the abode of the spirit and that of the body at the time of death?

REVELATION 20:13 _____

10. Who now holds the keys to both these realms?

REVELATION 1:18 _____

In the Old Testament we have the *Hebrew* word *Sheol* and in the New Testament the *Greek* word *Hades,* both siginfying the abode of departed spirits, whether saved or lost. Some translations fail to distinguish between the various words used in Scripture for the spirit world, thus causing much confusion in teaching. Both the Hebrew and Greek languages have completely different words for "grave." The word *Sheol* is never used in the plural for it is one place, whereas there are many graves. Scripture never speaks of an individual's *Sheol,* but we often read of an individual's grave. The body is never said to be in *Sheol* and the spirit or the soul are never said to be in the grave.

11. The abode of departed spirits, *Hades,* is described by Christ as being in two divisions prior to the finished work of the cross. Could those in the section assigned to the lost cross over to the section assigned to those who were saved?

LUKE 16:26 _____

_____

Hades is not the final hell. The contents of death (the grave) and *Hades* (the place of departed spirits) are to be emptied into hell on the final day (REVELATION 20:14).

Prior to Christ's death and resurrection, the spirit world is represented as being *below* and into it both saved and lost are said to have *descended.*

35

12. When the godly Samuel was called back from *Sheol* to pronounce judgment on Saul, did he come from above or from below?

I SAMUEL 28:11, 13, 15 _____

13. When Christ ascended on high what did He do with the waiting spirits in the Paradise section of the spirit world below?

EPHESIANS 4:8 _____

14. What had He done before He ascended taking this section of the lower spirit world with Him?

EPHESIANS 4:9 _____

15. Where did He go with those whom He led away in His triumphant train?

EPHESIANS 4:10 _____

16. Now that Christ ascended, do those who go to Paradise ascend or descend?

II CORINTHIANS 12:1-4 _____

Thus it is evident that the lower *Hades* has already been emptied of the redeemed. Only the lost still go there. The spirits of the saved go to be with Christ, awaiting the day of His return when they will be clothed with immortality. The spirits of the lost in that lower *Hades* await the day of judgment and in the meantime suffer conscious torment.

check-up time No. 7

What have you learned in this lesson? Review the lesson in the light of the self-check test below. Check carefully any questions you can't answer. Be sure you have filled in the blanks correctly. When you think you are ready, take the test without looking up the answers.

In the right-hand margin write "True" or "False" after each of the following statements.

1. At death the believer immediately receives his glorified body. _____

2. At death the immaterial part of man leaves the body. _____

3. The believer loses all conscious thinking power at death. _____

4. When a believer dies he goes to be with Christ. _____

5. The Bible carefully distinguishes between the abode of the body and the abode of the spirit at death. _____

6. Satan holds the keys of death. _____

7. The Lord indicated there was a strong possibility that those who were lost would be able to pass over eventually to be with those that are saved. _____

8. Now that Christ has ascended, those who go to be with Him at death likewise ascend. _____

9. Prior to Christ's ascension the believers descended into the abode of the dead. _____

10. The location of the believing dead appears to have been changed at the time of Christ's crucifixion. _____

Turn to page 64 and check your answers.

What Happens to the Unbeliever at Death?

From the Lord's teaching in LUKE 16:20-31 we learn that those who now go to *Hades* (*Sheol*), the intermediate abode of lost spirits, are in some degree of anguish (HEBREWS 10:27), although the final judgment will not be passed until the lost appear before the Great White Throne.

1. What was one of the things that tormented the rich man in *Hades?*

LUKE 16:23 _____

2. How did he describe his sensations in *Hades?*

LUKE 16:24 _____

_____

3. What did Abraham say to him?

LUKE 16:25 _____

_____

A remorseful memory will burn more intensely than any literal flame could scorch the body. Note that the rich man is said to have a sensation of suffering, although his body is said to have been left behind in the grave (LUKE 16:22).

4. With what are the disembodied spirits of the lost in *Sheol* surrounded? ("Hell" in this verse should be *Sheol*.)

II SAMUEL 22:6 _____

To say that there is no future retribution of the wicked is to ignore the plain statements of Scripture. Those with defective views of sin and weak conceptions of God may push aside the Bible teaching concerning future punishment of the wicked, saying that "God is love" and therefore could not cause suffering beyond this life. The Scripture, however, portrays God also as "a consuming fire." We may rest assured that whatever punishment is meted out to the lost will be consistent with infinite love and perfect justice.

5. After reading PSALM 73 would you say that there is any reasonable foundation for the view of some that all the hell to be experienced by the sinner is in this life?

_____

6. Who often suffers more affliction in this life than the wicked man?

PSALM 73:13, 14 _____

In studying what the Bible says about the final hell we must be careful not to take passages where the word "hell" occurs in our version but where the original is *Sheol* or *Hades*. The New Testament word used by Christ for the final hell is *Gehenna*. It is the Greek form of the Hebrew word *Ghi-Hinnom*, "Valley of Hinnom." In this valley, just outside of Jerusalem, the city refuse was cast and constant fires burned. Jesus took this valley as a type of the future retribution of those cast away from the presence of God. (The Old Testament Hebrew word for the same place was *Tophet*. See ISAIAH 30:33.)

7. Did Jesus hold out any hope for either soul or body of those who are cast into hell?

MATTHEW 10:28 _____

8. Is there any possibility of the wicked escaping the damnation of hell?

MATTHEW 23:33 _____

9. Is there any hell fire raging out in this world now?

JAMES 3:6 _____

Note that the word for "hell" in this verse is *Gehenna*.

10. Would it seem from this that hell fire is literal flame?

_____

11. What cities of earth are said to have suffered "the vengeance of eternal fire"?

II PETER 2:6; JUDE 7 _____

Note that while the smoke of Sodom's burning still ascends, the actual site of this city is said to lie beneath the waters of the Dead Sea. We are also told that the place was "overthrown in a moment" (LAMENTATIONS 4:6).

12. How does John describe the abode of the damned?

REVELATION 20:10-15 _____

The "lake of fire," referred to five times in REVELATION 19 and 20, occurs in a book largely consisting of symbolism. In view of the symbolic use of fire in other parts of the Bible, it might well be that the references to hell fire are an intense symbol of losing one's soul forever and the intense mental and spiritual agony resulting from this.

13. What is the Lord's warning to all those who are thoughtless concerning eternal realities?

MATTHEW 16:26 _____

_____

14. What will be God's basis of judgment for all those who reject the salvation He has freely provided in Christ?

REVELATION 20:12 _____

15. Are anybody's own works acceptable to God as a basis of salvation?

ROMANS 3:10, 12 _____

16. What is another reason why human merit is ruled out as a basis of salvation?

EPHESIANS 2:9 _____

17. On what basis then does God save men and women from hell?

EPHESIANS 2:8; ROMANS 6:23 _____

18. How can a person who has never trusted Christ know, even now, that he is heading for certain doom?

JOHN 3:18 _____

_____

19. How can a person who has trusted Christ know, even now, that he will not have to face the wrath of God?

JOHN 3:16 _____

_____

_____

20. What is your answer to this question: Have I truly accepted Christ as my personal Saviour?

_____

check-up time No. 8

What have you learned in this lesson? Review the lesson in the light of the self-check test below. Check carefully any questions you can't answer. Be sure you have filled in the blanks correctly. When you think you are ready, take the test without looking up the answers.

In the right-hand margin write "True" or "False" after each of the following statements.

1. In the place of torment the rich man was unconscious. _____

2. The lost are surrounded by comforts after death. _____

3. All the hell there is will be experienced in this life. _____

4. There is still hope for those who are cast into hell. _____

5. The cities that suffered the vengeance of eternal fire were Sodom and Gomorrah. _____

6. The abode of the damned is described as "a lake of fire." _____

7. The basis of judgment for those who have rejected Christ will be their works. _____

8. Some people's good works will keep them out of hell. _____

9. God's salvation is based on faith, not works. _____

10. There is an express promise in the Bible that those who trust Christ will not perish. _____

Turn to page 64 and check your answers.

The Great Tribulation

Following the rapture of true believers, the nations are to be plunged into a terrible period of upheaval and judgment. Prophetic references to the Great Tribulation, the seventieth week of Daniel, the day of the Lord and the time of Jacob's trouble, all seem to refer to the same general time.

1. What did Jesus say as to the coming Great Tribulation?

MATTHEW 24:21 _____

_____

2. What similar statements are made regarding the seventieth week of Daniel's prophecy?

DANIEL 9:27; 12:1 _____

_____

3. What did Joel say about the time of wrath known as the "day of the Lord"?

JOEL 2:1, 2 _____

_____

4. What did Jeremiah say regarding the sufferings of Israel in a coming day?

JEREMIAH 30:7 _____

_____

Daniel was told that God had allotted a period of seventy "weeks" (sevens) for the consummation of judgment upon Israel (DANIEL 9:24-27). Sixty-nine of those weeks of years (483 years) takes us from the time Cyrus issued his decree permitting the restoration and rebuilding of Jerusalem to the crucifixion of Christ. The seventieth week is suspended because of God's present dealings in grace through the Church. After the rapture of the Church, the seventieth week will run its course. The major portion of the book of Revelation is taken up with a detailed description of the judgments yet to come.

5. What race of people will be particularly affected by this coming consummation of events?

DANIEL 9:24 _____

6. What city will be prominent at this time?

DANIEL 9:24 _____

7. What awaits the Jews now returning to the land?

JEREMIAH 30:7-11 _____

_____

During this time of coming tribulation the world will be controlled by "a man of sin" (II THESSALONIANS 2:3), also known as the Antichrist and termed in Revelation as the "Beast" (REVELATION 13:1). The Antichrist will make a seven year covenant with Israel (the last "week" of Daniel), which he will suddenly violate when it has only half expired. This last half of Daniel's seventieth week is referred to as "time, times and half a time" (REVELATION 12:14); "forty and two months" (REVELATION 11:2; 13:5) and "a thousand, two hundred and three score days" (REVELATION 11:3; 12:6).

8. Having rejected Christ, who will the Jews be ready to receive once they have assembled back in the land?

JOHN 5:43; DANIEL 9:27 _____

9. How will they be disillusioned in the midst of the seven years?

REVELATION 11:7; II THESSALONIANS 2:3-4 _____

_____

10. Will they be left without a witness in those days?

REVELATION 11:3-7 _____

11. What action will the Beast take in connection with the ceremonies being conducted in the rebuilt temple?

DANIEL 9:27; 11:31 _____

_____

12. What will he demand that the whole world do?

REVELATION 13:14; II THESSALONIANS 2:3-4 _____

13. Who will be cast down to earth in the midst of the tribulation period?

REVELATION 12:7-12; 13:5 _____

14. For how long will the Beast be able to completely control things?

DANIEL 7:25 _____

15. What will every individual be compelled to receive before being permitted to buy or sell?

REVELATION 13:16 _____

16. What will happen to those who refuse to worship the Beast?

REVELATION 13:15 _____

17. What proportion of Jews will live through these days of terror?

ZECHARIAH 13:8, 9 _____

18. How many of Israel's tribes will be sealed as special witnesses of the Lord during the Tribulation period?

REVELATION 7:4 _____

19. Will there be any Gentiles saved during this time?

REVELATION 7:9-14 _____

20. What great gathering will mark the climax of the Great Tribulation?

REVELATION 16:14-16 _____

21. Against whom is this war directed in particular?

REVELATION 17:14 _____

22. What will happen to the following:

a. Antichrist? II THESSALONIANS 2:8 _____

b. The False Prophet? REVELATION 19:20 _____

c. Satan? REVELATION 20:3 _____

check-up time No. 9

What have you learned in this lesson? Review the lesson in the light of the self-check test below. Check carefully any questions you can't answer. Be sure you have filled in the blanks correctly. When you think you are ready, take the test without looking up the answers.

In the right-hand margin write "True" or "False" after each of the following statements.

1. The Great Tribulation is going to be a time of trouble without parallel in human history. _____

2. The Great Tribulation is described as "the time of Jacob's trouble." _____

3. The race most particularly affected by the Great Tribulation will be the Russians. _____

4. The city that will figure largely in the Great Tribulation is described as "the holy city." _____

5. The Jews will accept the Antichrist as their Messiah. _____

6. For their refusal to obey God, the Jews will be left without a witness in the coming of trouble. _____

7. The image of the Beast, the Antichrist, will be set up in the temple in a coming day. _____

8. One hundred and forty-four thousand Jews will be divinely sealed as special witnesses during the Tribulation. _____

9. Very few Gentiles will be saved during this period. _____

10. The Tribulation will climax in the Battle of Armageddon. _____

Turn to page 64 and check your answers.

Palestine and the Jews

Frederick the Great of Prussia once asked his chaplain to defend the inspiration of the Bible. He responded simply, "The Jews, Sire." No one can explain the remarkable history of the Jews apart from the Bible.

The earliest promise concerning this nation was made to Abraham (GENESIS 13:16). The nation's sojourn and slavery in Egypt and subsequent exodus were also foretold to him (GENESIS 15: 13, 14).

1. On their deliverance from Egypt and just prior to their possession of Palestine, what did Moses prophesy concerning their history in the promised land?

DEUTERONOMY 31:20, 21 _____

_____

2. How did Moses predict their eventual world-wide dispersal centuries before they became a great people?

DEUTERONOMY 28:63, 64 _____

_____

3. How was their remarkable resistance to absorption into other nations predicted?

NUMBERS 23:9 _____

4. How were their sufferings among the nations foretold?

DEUTERONOMY 28:65-67 _____

_____

5. What did Christ say that the outcome of their rejection of Him would mean to the Jews?

Luke 19:41-44; 21:24 _____

_____

6. What part of Israel is not shut out from the spiritual blessings in Christ?

Romans 11:5-7 _____

7. In what way is the present return of the Jews to Palestine an event of great prophetic significance?

Jeremiah 23:7, 8 _____

_____

8. How did Ezekiel foresee the regathering of Israel in the last days?

Ezekiel 37:11-14 _____

_____

9. What did Jeremiah say of the spiritual condition of the Jews when the regathering is finally fully accomplished?

Jeremiah 31:31-34 _____

_____

10. What will transpire to bring about the conversion of the Jews to Christ in spite of the unbelief in which they return to the land?

Ezekiel 22:17-22; Zechariah 14:2, 3; Jeremiah 30:6, 7 _____

_____

11. Who will defeat the forces of the Antichrist under whom anti-Semitism will reach its height?

ZECHARIAH 14:3, 4; REVELATION 19:11-18 _____

_____

12. To what spot will Christ return to effect the deliverance and conversion of Israel?

ZECHARIAH 14:4 _____

13. How will the Jews react to the Lord's return at this time?

ZECHARIAH 12:10; JEREMIAH 31:9 _____

_____

14. Once the Lord's reign is established, how will the Gentiles react?

ZECHARIAH 8:20-23 _____

_____

The history of Israel is inseparable from the land of Canaan and Palestine. It was given to Abraham and his seed forever, and while the Gentiles have seized upon it, Israel has the true title, recorded in the Word of God.

15. How did Moses describe God's regard for this land?

DEUTERONOMY 11:12 _____

_____

16. In what condition was the land to lie so long as Israel was scattered among the nations?

DEUTERONOMY 29:22-28 _____

_____

Since the fall of Jerusalem in A.D. 70, many peoples have tried to restore Palestine, but without success. Its desolation has continued until the advent of the Zionist movement. It should also be remembered that the territory given to Abraham has never been fully occupied. It will extend from the Nile to the Euphrates (GENESIS 15:18). Its measurements are given in EZEKIEL 47:13-23. It lies between five great seas like the hub of a wheel: the Mediterranean, the Red Sea, the Persian Gulf, the Caspian Sea and the Nile. This vast area is now largely desert, but in a coming day it will blossom as the rose. It lies in a key relationship to three continents Europe, Africa and Asia. Great physical changes are yet to take place (EZEKIEL 47:1-12; ZECHARIAH 14).

17. What will become of ancient cities, long in ruins?

EZEKIEL 36:9, 10 _____

18. What city is to be the capital of Israel?

II CHRONICLES 6:6 _____

19. What did Jesus predict about this city?

LUKE 21:24 _____

20. What is to be the future of this city?

ISAIAH 62:2-4 _____

_____

21. What new name will be given to this city during the earthly reign of Christ?

JEREMIAH 33:16 _____

*What have you learned in this lesson? Review the
lesson in the light of the self-check test below. Check
carefully any questions you can't answer. Be sure
you have filled in the blanks correctly. When you
think you are ready, take the test without looking
up the answers.*

*In the right-hand margin write "True" or "False"
after each of the following statements.*

1. Before they even possessed the promised land,
Moses prophesied the apostasy of Israel. _____

2. The inability of the world's peoples to assimilate
the Jews was foreseen by the Gentile prophet Ba-
laam. _____

3. The Lord Jesus declared that Israel's rejection of
Him would bring untold sufferings upon the nation. _____

4. The rejection of Christ is endorsed by all Jews. _____

5. The present return of the Jews to Palestine is without any prophetic significance. _____

6. Ezekiel's vision of the valley of dry bones depicts
the regathering and rebirth of the nation of Israel. _____

7. The Great Tribulation will harden the Jews against
Christ more than ever. _____

8. Christ is going to return to the Mount of Olives to
bring about the deliverance and conversion of Israel. _____

9. Once the Lord's reign is established, the Gentiles
will despise the Jews. _____

10. The capital city of Christ's empire will be Rome. _____

Turn to page 64 and check your answers.

The Coming False Messiah

Some important trinities of Scripture

1. Who comprises the divine Trinity?

MATTHEW 28:19, 20 _____   _____

2. How does man reflect the trinity of God?

I THESSALONIANS 5:23 _____

3. What trinity now opposes the work of God?

I JOHN 2:16 _____   _____

4. What trinity will bring evil to its culmination in the Tribulation period?

REVELATION 20:10 _____

A personal Antichrist

Some think that references to the coming Antichrist have to do with a *system* of evil but deny that there will be a personal Antichrist.

5. What does Paul say about this?

II THESSALONIANS 2:3 _____

_____

Compare also II THESSALONIAN 2:3, 8; REVELATION 13:4, 18. It should be noted that the Antichrist is often referred to with a personal pronoun. The sin of man will head up at last in a "man of sin."

6. How wide will be the Antichrist's influence?

REVELATION 13:3, 4 _____

7. What will be his chief characteristics?

REVELATION 13:5, 6; DANIEL 11:36 _____

_____

8. For whom will he have a particular hatred?

REVELATION 13:7 _____

9. How many will be compelled to worship him or else be slain?

REVELATION 13:8 _____

10. How long will he continue in power after his manifestation?

REVELATION 13:5 _____

The False Prophet

11. Who does the False Prophet, called the second Beast, fully support?

REVELATION 13:12 _____

Some believe the second Beast to be the Antichrist because he has "horns like a lamb." However, the first Beast is foremost in opposition to Christ and the saints, while this second, lamblike Beast directs all attention and worship to the first Beast. The second Beast is a religious leader whose work will be to bring the cults and religions of the world into the ranks of the Antichrist.

12. How will the False Prophet gain the attention of religious people?

REVELATION 13:13, 14 _____

13. What will all be compelled to wear as a badge of loyalty to the Antichrist?

REVELATION 13:16, 17 _____

14. What is "the number" of the Antichrist's name?

REVELATION 13:18 _____

The number six, in Scripture, is associated with man. It is one short of seven, the number of perfection, and is associated with sin. Here it is multiplied by tens and hundreds and stands for the great trinity of evil.

Contrasts between Christ and Antichrist

15. From whence did Christ come?

JOHN 6:38 _____

16. From whence will the Antichrist come?

REVELATION 11:7 _____

17. What was characteristic of Christ?

PHILIPPIANS 2:8 _____

18. What will be characteristic of Antichrist?

II THESSALONIANS 2:4 _____

19. How was Christ received?

ISAIAH 53:3 _____

20. How will the world receive the Antichrist?

REVELATION 13:3, 4 _____

21. Where did Christ go when His work was done?

MARK 16:19 _____

22. Where will Antichrist go at the last?

REVELATION 17:8-11 _____

The origin and overthrow of the Antichrist

DANIEL 11:37 is frequently quoted as evidence that the Antichrist will be a Jew. The marginal reading of this verse renders "God of his fathers" as "gods of his fathers," indicating that he will have no regard for any religious beliefs whatsoever. He *may* be a Jew, but there are passages which seem to indicate otherwise.

From DANIEL 8 it would seem that he is to arise from one of the four divisions of Alexander's broken empire. From the great image vision of DANIEL 2 it has been widely understood that the Beast will be the last representative of *Gentile* power on the earth. LUKE 21:24 seems to support this. This superman who is to claim both religious and political supremacy is to revive, it would seem, all the perished glory of the previous world empires of the Gentiles. It would seem from I JOHN 2:18-22 that he is more likely to be an apostate Christian than an apostate Jew. Some say, "Is it likely that the Jews would accept as their Messiah one who is a Gentile?" It might equally be asked, "Would the Gentiles, in a day of universal anti-Semitism, unite in rendering homage and worship to one who is a Jew?

23. Will the great power of the Antichrist finally be broken?

DANIEL 8:25 _____

24. What will prove to be his destruction?

II THESSALONIANS 2:8 _____

check-up time No. 11

What have you learned in this lesson? Review the lesson in the light of the self-check test below. Check carefully any questions you can't answer. Be sure you have filled in the blanks correctly. When you think you are ready, take the test without looking up the answers.

In the right-hand margin write "True" or "False" after each of the following statements.

1. The devil, the Antichrist and the False Prophet will comprise the coming trinity of evil. _____

2. The Antichrist's influence will be limited to Palestine. _____

3. The Antichrist will have a particular love for the people who believe in God. _____

4. The Antichrist's reign is to last for a thousand years. _____

5. The False Prophet fully supports the Antichrist. _____

6. The "mark of the beast" referred to in Scripture is gluttony. _____

7. The number of Antichrist's name is 666. _____

8. The world will acclaim Antichrist. _____

9. The Antichrist will be characterized by humility. _____

10. Antichrist's doom is to be cast into the bottomless pit. _____

Turn to page 64 and check your answers.

The Millennial Kingdom

The word "Millennium" means "thousand years" and gets its Scripture basis from statements in the book of Revelation in which a thousand years' reign of Christ on earth is predicted.

1. What does God intend to do when all earthly kingdoms fall?

DANIEL 2:44 _____

2. In what sphere will the coming King reign and prosper?

JEREMIAH 23:5 _____

3. Who will this King be?

ISAIAH 24:23; MICAH 4:7 _____

4. Where will the seat of His government be?

ISAIAH 24:23; MICAH 4:7 _____

5. Will this kingdom be established through the preaching of the gospel, by a process of evolution, or as a result of force?

MATTHEW 24:30; DANIEL 2:34, 35; REVELATION 11:15 _____

_____

6. Will Christ's authority be shared with any rulers of earth?

ZECHARIAH 14:9; PSALM 72:11 _____

7. Will any part of the earth be outside His authority?

PSALM 72:8; ZECHARIAH 9:10 _____

8. Who will receive places of authority under the King?

JUDE 14, 15; REVELATION 3:21; 5:9, 10; 20:4 _____

_____

9. What will Christ do for the remnant of Israel?

EZEKIEL 20:33-38; AMOS 9:9, 10 _____

_____

10. Will there be any more heathen when Christ reigns?

PSALM 47:5-9 _____

_____

11. What will happen to the wild beasts?

ISAIAH 65:25; 11:6-9; HOSEA 2:18 _____

_____

12. Can there be any wars during this era?

ISAIAH 2:1-4 _____

13. Will it be difficult to secure justice?

PSALM 72:1-8 _____

14. What will happen to those with physical handicaps?

ISAIAH 35:5, 6 _____

15. What will happen to earth's vast desert regions during the reign of Christ?

Isaiah 35:1, 7 _____

16. Will there be any change in man's normal life span on earth during this age?

Isaiah 65:20 _____

17. What will happen to those who deliberately sin during this coming time?

Isaiah 65:20 _____

While the curse upon nature is to be removed during the Millennium, the effects of the curse will not be brought to an end until the "new heavens and new earth" are created after the Millennium is over. The Millennium will be a period of blessedness such as this earth has never seen, but during this period children will be born into the world as now and will need to be redeemed. The new birth will be as essential then as it is now. During the Millennium Christ will reign "with a rod of iron," implying that the effects of the curse are held in restraint by divine power. As soon as this restraint is temporarily removed, we read of a fresh rebellion against God.

18. Who will be released at the end of the Millennium, and for how long?

Revelation 20:7 _____

19. What will happen to those who join this last rebellion against Christ?

Revelation 20:8, 9 _____

_____

This brief, mad undertaking will be quickly ended by God. One sentence tells the story (REVELATION 20:9). We then go on to read of the new eternal order which will never be invaded by sin —whether arising from the world, the flesh or the devil.

20. What did the Lord Jesus say was essential to those wishing to see His kingdom?

JOHN 3:3 _____

21. To whom were these words originally spoken?

JOHN 3:1, 2 _____

22. Of what highly favored nation was this man?

JOHN 3:1 _____

23. What three things are we told "being born of God" is *not?*
JOHN 1:13

a. _____

b. _____

c. _____

24. What had His own nation done to Christ?

JOHN 1:11 _____

25. In what way can a person be born again and thus qualify for a place in the kingdom of God?

JOHN 1:12 _____

_____

26. Do you qualify? _____

_____

check-up time No. 12

What have you learned in this lesson? Review the lesson in the light of the self-check test below. Check carefully any questions you can't answer. Be sure you have filled in the blanks correctly. When you think you are ready, take the test without looking up the answers.

In the right-hand margin write "True" or "False" after each of the following statements.

1. God is ultimately going to establish His own kingdom here on earth. _____

2. Christ's kingdom is going to be established on earth by force. _____

3. The "uttermost parts of the north" will be outside the dominion of Christ. _____

4. The wild beasts will have their natures changed when Christ reigns on earth. _____

5. During the reign of Christ war will be abolished. _____

6. The vast desert regions of earth will be maintained as relics of the former curse during Christ's reign. _____

7. The average life span for man during Christ's reign will be lengthened to one hundred years. _____

8. At the end of the Millennium, Satan will be released from his prison. _____

9. Although Satan will be able to foment a worldwide rebellion against Christ at the end of the Millennium, his success will be short-lived. _____

10. Apart from an experience of the new birth, no man can even see the kingdom of God. _____

Turn to page 64 and check your answers.

Suggestions for class use

1. The class teacher may wish to tear this page from each workbook as the answer key is on the reverse side.

2. The teacher should study the lesson first, filling in the blanks in the workbook. He should be prepared to give help to the class on some of the harder places in the lesson. He should also take the self-check tests himself, check his answers with the answer key and look up any question answered incorrectly.

3. Class sessions can be supplemented by the teacher's giving a talk or leading a discussion on the subject to be studied. The class could then fill in the workbook together as a group, in teams, or individually. If so desired by the teacher, however, this could be done at home. The self-check tests can be done as homework by the class.

4. The self-check tests can be corrected at the beginning of each class session. A brief discussion of the answers can serve as review for the previous lesson.

5. The teacher should motivate and encourage his students. Some public recognition might well be given to class members who successfully complete this course.

answer key

to self-check tests

Be sure to look up any questions you answered incorrectly.

Q gives the number of the test *question*.

A gives the correct *answer*.

R *refers* you back to the number of the question in the lesson itself, where the correct answer is to be found.

Mark with an "x" your wrong answers.

Q	TEST 1 A	TEST 1 R	TEST 2 A	TEST 2 R	TEST 3 A	TEST 3 R	TEST 4 A	TEST 4 R	TEST 5 A	TEST 5 R	TEST 6 A	TEST 6 R
1	T	2	F	1	F	1	F	3	F	2	F	2
2	F	3	F	4	T	2	T	6	T	3	T	3
3	F	7	T	5	T	4	T	7	T	4	T	6
4	T	17	F	6	T	5	T	8	T	6	T	9
5	F	18	T	8	T	5	F	9	T	10	F	11
6	F	20	T	11	F	6	T	12	F	13	T	17
7	T	25	F	13	T	8	F	13	T	15	T	20
8	T	27	T	14	F	9	T	14	F	16	F	22
9	T	28	T	3	F	11	F	17	F	18	F	23
10	T	4	T	7	T	12	T	19	T	19	T	25

Q	TEST 7 A	TEST 7 R	TEST 8 A	TEST 8 R	TEST 9 A	TEST 9 R	TEST 10 A	TEST 10 R	TEST 11 A	TEST 11 R	TEST 12 A	TEST 12 R
1	F	1	F	2	T	2	T	1	T	4	T	1
2	T	4	F	4	T	4	T	3	F	6	T	5
3	F	5	F	5	F	5	T	5	F	8	F	7
4	T	6	F	7	T	6	F	6	F	10	T	11
5	T	9	T	11	T	8	F	7	T	11	T	12
6	F	10	T	12	F	10	T	8	F	13	F	15
7	F	11	T	14	T	11	F	10	T	14	F	16
8	T	16	F	15	T	18	T	12	T	20	T	18
9	T	12	T	17	F	19	F	14	F	18	T	19
10	F	13	T	19	T	20	F	18	F	22	T	20

how well did you do?

0-1 wrong answers—excellent work

2-3 wrong answers—review errors carefully

4 or more wrong answers—restudy the lesson before going on to the next one